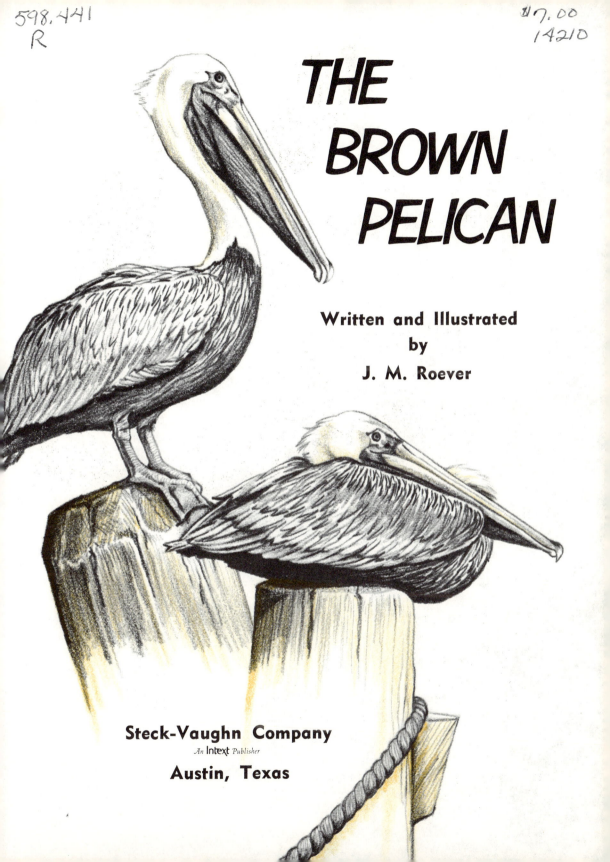

THE
BROWN
PELICAN

Written and Illustrated
by
J. M. Roever

Steck-Vaughn Company
An Intext Publisher
Austin, Texas

Library of Congress Cataloging in Publication Data

Roever, J. M.

The brown pelican.
(Steck-Vaughn wildlife series)

SUMMARY: Describes the appearance, behavior, life cycle, and ecological relationships of the brown pelican, now an endangered species.

1. Brown pelican—Juvenile literature. [1. Brown pelican. 2. Pelicans] I. Title.

QL696.P47R63   598.4'41   74-10982

ISBN 0-8114-7766-5

Library of Congress Catalog Card Number 74-10982

The Brown Pelican

Whether flying in tight formation, somersaulting and nose-diving into the sea, begging scraps from fishing boats, or sunning on wooden pier pilings, brown pelicans are a fascinating and entertaining sight.

In 1970, the government added the brown pelican's name to the list of endangered animals. Today, nature's famous flying fisherman, the brown pelican, is steadily disappearing from the seashore.

The Two North American Pelicans

Fossils of ancient pelicans reveal that these birds have barely changed in the past 30 to 40 million years. Many species (<u>spee</u>-sheez), or types of pelicans, are already extinct (ex-<u>stinkt</u>).

There are 8 species of pelicans living today. Six types of white pelicans are native to the Old World. One other white pelican is found in the New World. The brown pelican, the smallest species, occurs only in the New World.

The two North American pelicans differ greatly from each other in appearance, size, habits, and home range. Brown pelicans are seaside birds and seek their food in salt water. White pelicans are inland birds, fishing in fresh water except in winter when they fly south to coastal areas. Then flocks of brown and white pelicans occasionally are seen resting on sandbars or flying together.

Fossils are the hardened remains or impressions of animals or plants that lived long ago.

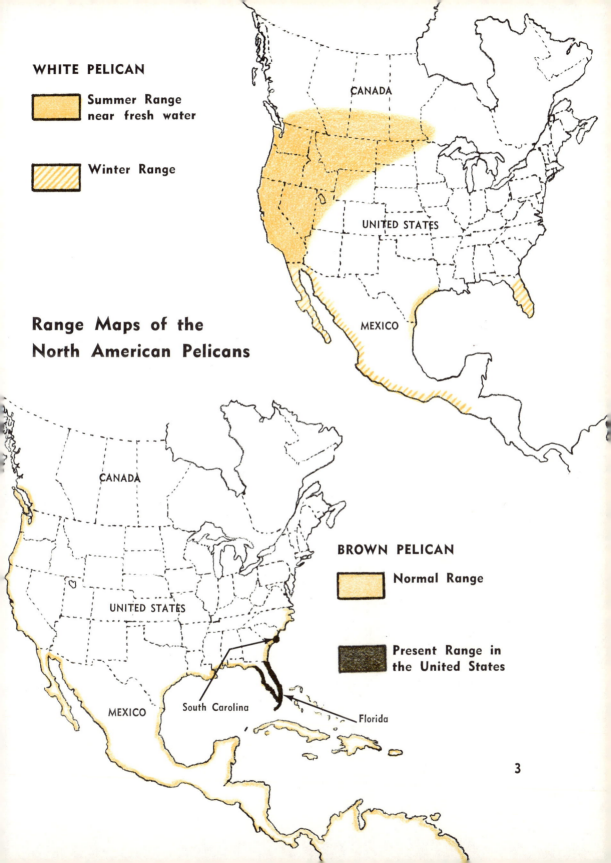

WHITE PELICAN

Summer Range near fresh water

Winter Range

CANADA

UNITED STATES

MEXICO

Range Maps of the North American Pelicans

CANADA

UNITED STATES

MEXICO

BROWN PELICAN

Normal Range

Present Range in the United States

South Carolina

Florida

3

Recognizing the Brown Pelican

The adult brown pelican isn't really brown. The feathers on top of its wings and back are silvery gray. Its underparts vary in tones of light and dark gray. In winter the brown pelican's face and the crown of its head are yellow. Its white neck ends in a bib of golden feathers. In summer an elegant collar of velvety brown feathers encircles the pelican's curved neck. The golden facial feathers are replaced with snowy white ones.

The immature brown pelican is better suited to its name. The feathers on top of its wings and back are various shades of brown. The head and neck feathers are dark brown, but its underparts are white. When the pelican reaches its third year, adult feathers replace the brown plumage. Male and female pelicans look alike. It is not possible to identify them by feathers, color, or size.

Adult Brown Pelican
(summer plumage)

**Immature
Brown
Pelican**

**Adult Brown Pelican
(winter plumage)**

Classification

All over the world, scientists classify, or identify, animals by Latin names. A brown pelican's identification tag would look like this.

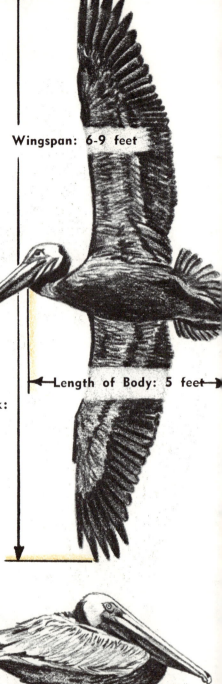

Wingspan: 6-9 feet

Length of Body: 5 feet

Length of Beak: 12 inches

Class—Aves (*ay-veez*), Latin word for birds
Order—Pelecaniformes (pel-eh-can-i-*for*-meez), "the ancient pelicanlike birds"
Scientific Family Name—Pelecanidae (pel-eh-*can*-i-dee), "the pelicans"
Genus and Species—Pelecanus occidentalis (pel-eh-*can*-us ox-i-*den*-tal-is), "pelican of the western world"
Common Name—brown pelican

6

Average Adult Brown Pelican

Pounds

The identification tag of the American white pelican would look like this.

Length of Beak: 12 inches

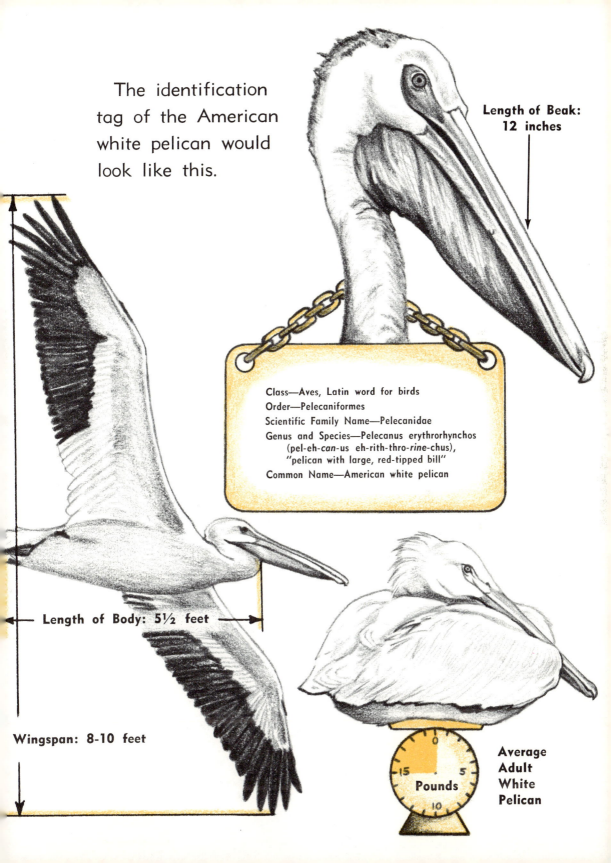

Class—Aves, Latin word for birds
Order—Pelecaniformes
Scientific Family Name—Pelecanidae
Genus and Species—Pelecanus erythrorhynchos
    (pel-eh-*can*-us eh-rith-thro-*rine*-chus),
    "pelican with large, red-tipped bill"
Common Name—American white pelican

Length of Body: 5½ feet

Wingspan: 8-10 feet

Pounds

Average Adult White Pelican

The Flying Fisherman

Nature has provided the pelican with three fine pieces of fishing equipment. Its wide, webbed feet serve as paddles. Its air-filled body becomes a floating life preserver, and its strange beak converts to a handy dip net.

The brown pelican and all its relatives are known as totipalmate (tod-tuh-<u>pol</u>-mate), or "oar-footed" birds. Webbed skin connects all four toes of the pelican's foot. Other web-footed birds, such as ducks, have only three toes connected, and the hind toe hangs free.

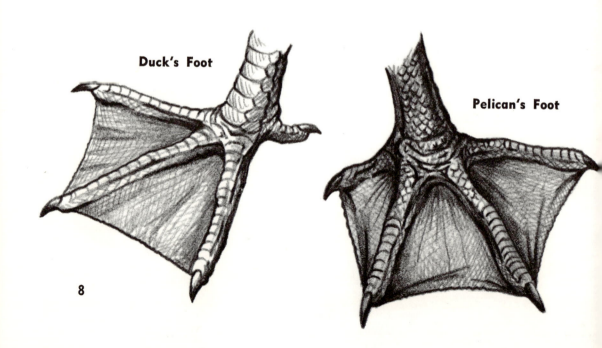

Duck's Foot

Pelican's Foot

8

How the Pelican Flies

On land the brown pelican appears awkward and clownish. It seems to trip over its own floppy webbed feet. In order to fly, the pelican builds up speed by hopping—feet together—along the ground. A swimming pelican takes off by pattering its feet across the surface of the water. The pelican's huge wings slice through the air until one final push of the webbed feet launches the bird skyward.

Clumsiness gives way to dignity and skill as the brown pelican flies. The head, neck, and long beak are tucked back against the pelican's shoulders, and the graceful sea bird glides along with slow, powerful wingbeats.

The Air-Filled Pelican

The shafts, or center ribs, of a pelican's feathers are hollow and full of air. The long, round bones of the pelican's legs and wings are also hollow, and beneath the pelican's skin is a network of air pockets. Long, thin tubes run to the hollow bones and air sacs from the pelican's lungs. When the pelican flies, air is pumped into the lungs, bones, and air sacs by the steady beat of the great bird's wings.

Hollow Shaft

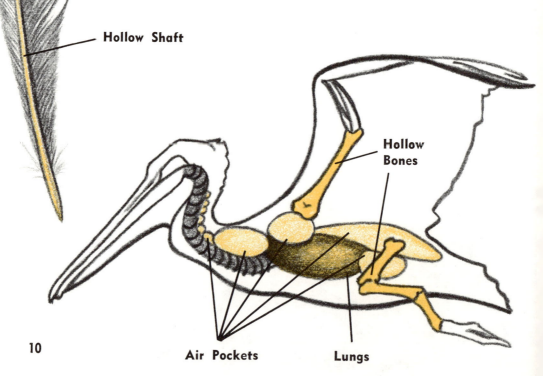

Hollow Bones

Air Pockets

Lungs

The air trapped within a pelican's body helps to keep the bird aloft as it sweeps over the waves in search of fish. When the pelican spies a meal, it dives into the water with wings half folded. It may dive from heights 60 or 70 feet above the water.

As the pelican hits the water, the air in its body acts as a cushion against the shock. The pelican does not dive deep into the water. In a few seconds it pops to the surface and then rocks gently on the waves like an inflated beach toy.

Pelicans are sociable birds. They fish, fly, rest, and even build nests close to the company of their companions. When pelicans fly together they dip, soar, and flap their wings one after the other as if playing follow-the-leader.

When the wind is pushing them from behind, pelicans fly high above the water. If they must fly into the wind, the great birds skim low over the waves where the wind is less forceful.

The Pelican's Dip Net Pouch

The brown pelican catches fish in the split second that it dives into the waves. Fastened to the flying fisherman's lower beak and neck is an elastic pouch of skin. Underwater, the pelican opens its beak, spreads its enormous pouch, and scoops up almost three gallons of fish and water.

On the surface again, the pelican tilts its head high, tips its beak low, and allows the water to drain out of the dip net pouch.

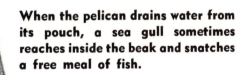

When the pelican drains water from its pouch, a sea gull sometimes reaches inside the beak and snatches a free meal of fish.

13

The pelican does not use its pouch to carry fish from one place to another but swallows each fish whole while floating on the waves. The long beak is tilted back, and the trapped fish slide down the great bird's throat. As much as four pounds of fish may be consumed in one day.

Scientists have observed that the pelican's pouch also helps to keep the sea bird cool in summer. Excess heat escapes from the pelican's body through the bare skin of the pouch. The large bird seems to be panting as the folds of skin tremble and vibrate beneath the long beak.

Only brown pelicans sky-dive for food.
When white pelicans go fishing they swim
side by side in a curved line. Beating
the water with their wings, the hungry
birds drive fish before them into shallow
water. Then white pelicans sweep their
scooped beaks back and forth through
the churning water and dip up the
trapped fish.

Life History of the Brown Pelican

On some remote island, a flock of brown pelicans establishes a nesting colony. Many other species of birds build their nests and roost or sleep on the same island as the pelicans. These nesting areas are known as "rookeries." For sea and shore birds they are safe refuges from the disturbances of humans and animals.

Mated adult pelicans build their nest together. Some nests are merely shallow holes scooped out of the ground and lined with a few twigs and shore plants. Other nests are constructed of sticks in the branches of low trees and bushes.

Although baby pelicans have been seen on nests all year round, the main nesting season is from February through September. The adult pelicans take turns incubating their 1 to 4 white eggs for 29 to 30 days.

An Island Rookery

Wood Storks

Great Blue Heron

Common Egret

Cattle Egret

White Ibis

Black Skimmers

Brown Pelican

A newly hatched pelican chick is sightless, feeble, and extremely ugly. Its naked skin is blood red, and it resembles a tiny prehistoric monster. In 2 or 3 days soft white down begins to cover the chick's body. But it still must be constantly protected from sun, wind, rain, and flying insects by the sheltering wings and body of the parent pelican.

Feeding baby pelicans is an endless task for the adults. One at a time they fly off to locate, catch, and swallow a few pouchfuls of fish. As each parent returns to the nest, it regurgitates (reh-ger-jih-tayts), or brings up, a portion of the consumed fish. At first the feeble nestling is barely able to lift its head, and the adult pelican must dribble food from its massive beak into the tiny beak of the hungry chick.

As soon as it is strong enough, the nestling learns to reach into the dip net pouch of the adult pelican. There the chick finds a meal of regurgitated fish waiting for it. But as the nestling grows, it becomes more demanding and aggressive about its mealtimes. Soon the nestling's entire head disappears into the parent's open mouth as it reaches far into the pouch for the eagerly awaited fish.

Although adult pelicans are silent, the nestlings grunt and bleat like lambs. When they are about 5 weeks old, the chicks born in ground nests begin to walk around. They congregate with other youngsters in small bands known as "pods." However, the chicks hatched in tree nests are confined to their upstairs living quarters until they are able to fly—at an age of about 9 weeks.

Before it reaches flying age, each pelican chick is fed almost 150 pounds of fish by its hardworking parents. As soon as young pelicans have learned to fly, they are known as fledglings (flej-lings).

Although they join the flock and gradually learn pelican fishing techniques, fledglings often pursue adult birds and continue to beg for food. By the time they are 4 months old, young pelicans are fully able to care for themselves.

Mullet

Some Food of Brown Pelicans

Menhaden

Crab

Pelicans usually eat fish unfit for human food.

"The Pelican in Her Piety"

In the Middle Ages the pelican's unusual method of feeding her nestlings led to a strange myth. Ancient observers believed the pelican was nourishing the chicks with blood from deep within her breast. The red tint on the tip of a pelican's beak was said to prove that the bird punctured its own breast to provide lifeblood for the young. Others claimed that if the pelican nestlings died, blood from the adult bird restored them to life.

So the symbol of "The Pelican in Her Piety" was used on banners and coats of arms to represent holiness, charity, love, and devotion to family.

"The Pelican in Her Piety"

Louisiana State Seal

The seal shows the pelican protecting her young. The pelican is Louisiana's state bird.

23

The Plight of the Brown Pelican

Although pelicans may live as long as 30 years, they face many hazards. About half of the young pelicans born in each colony do not survive. A hurricane's high waters occasionally wash away nests and young. Predatory fish and birds also take their toll. But like many other wild creatures, the pelican's worst enemies are humans.

About 75 years ago, fashionable ladies wore hats trimmed with bird plumes. Pelicans and many other birds were killed for their feathers. Boaters with guns often shot pelicans for sport.

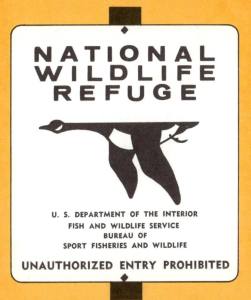

NATIONAL WILDLIFE REFUGE

U. S. DEPARTMENT OF THE INTERIOR
FISH AND WILDLIFE SERVICE
BUREAU OF
SPORT FISHERIES AND WILDLIFE

UNAUTHORIZED ENTRY PROHIBITED

ATLANTIC
OCEAN

Cape
Canaveral

East Coast
of Florida

Indian River

Sebastian
Inlet

Pelican
Island
National
Wildlife
Refuge

In 1903, hearing of the pelican's
plight, President Theodore Roosevelt
established the nation's very first federal
wildlife refuge. It was called "Pelican
Island"—a 3-acre sanctuary located in the
Indian River on Florida's east coast. But
the refuge did not always protect the
sea birds from human destruction.
During World War I hysterical rumors
claimed that pelicans ate fish needed
for hungry citizens. One night hundreds
of pelicans were clubbed to death on
the Pelican Island rookery.

25

Rain

Poison flows into the waterways of our nation. Eventually, poison enters the oceans.

Poisons in the Environment

Since the end of World War II, a new crisis has been affecting the brown pelicans and all other living creatures. Newly invented chemical herbicides and pesticides are used to control plant, animal, and insect pests.

When certain chemicals, such as DDT, are sprayed into the environment, they do not fade away. They are known as "persistent" or "hard pesticides." Rain washes hard chemicals into our waterways. When contaminated water evaporates, particles of hard pesticides enter into the air and may float to unsprayed areas thousands of miles away.

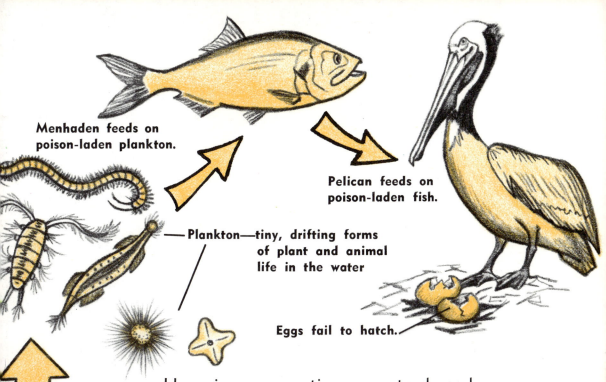

Menhaden feeds on poison-laden plankton.

Pelican feeds on poison-laden fish.

Plankton—tiny, drifting forms of plant and animal life in the water

Eggs fail to hatch.

Here is an aquatic, or water-based, food chain. Hard chemicals are absorbed by plankton low on the chain. The pesticide is stored, transferred, and multiplied in the fatty tissues of each higher animal in the chain.

Persistent pesticides cause chemical imbalance in an animal's reproductive system. Many brown pelicans lay eggs with shells too thin to protect developing chicks. Eggs have been found with no shells around them at all. Other eggs never hatch. Many pelican chicks are sickly and die within a few days.

27

Nesting colonies of brown pelicans have disappeared from the coasts of California, Texas, Mississippi, and Louisiana. Today only 24 nesting colonies remain—2 are in South Carolina, and 22 are in Florida.

Hard pesticides imperil all fish-eating animals. Pelicans, bald eagles, whooping cranes, ospreys, and sea lions are having difficulty raising young to carry on their species. Unfortunately, no one can tell how long that persistent pesticides will remain on our planet earth.

Dragonflies feast on mosquitoes.

Biological Control, A Safer Way

Praying mantises eat many insect pests.

Ladybugs destroy harmful aphids.

Wasps kill destructive caterpillars and moths.

28

Protecting Endangered Species

Many dedicated people are trying to help endangered species. They mark birds and animals with bands and colored plastic tags, or by attaching electronic tracking equipment to them. They keep records of birth, death, and animal behavior. Some species are being raised in captivity. Fledgling brown pelicans have been shipped from successful nesting areas to states where the great sea birds have vanished.

The strong odor of marigolds keeps many insects out of vegetable gardens.

Scientists are searching for safe ways to control plant, animal, and insect pests. Biological control is a wise method. Beneficial insects are released into areas where they destroy harmful insects. Natural ingredients such as plant juices are being used to manufacture pesticides.

29

The painted daisy is the source of a natural insecticide.

More than a century ago, Henry David Thoreau, a pioneer conservationist, warned that thoughtless humans must not be allowed to destroy our nation's wild inheritance. He wrote, "We all have need of nature," and "In wildness is the preservation of the world."

You can help to preserve our natural world if you join conservation groups and read wildlife magazines and books. Learn all that you can about nature and speak up if you see misuse of wilderness areas or wild creatures.